My Personal Hygiene

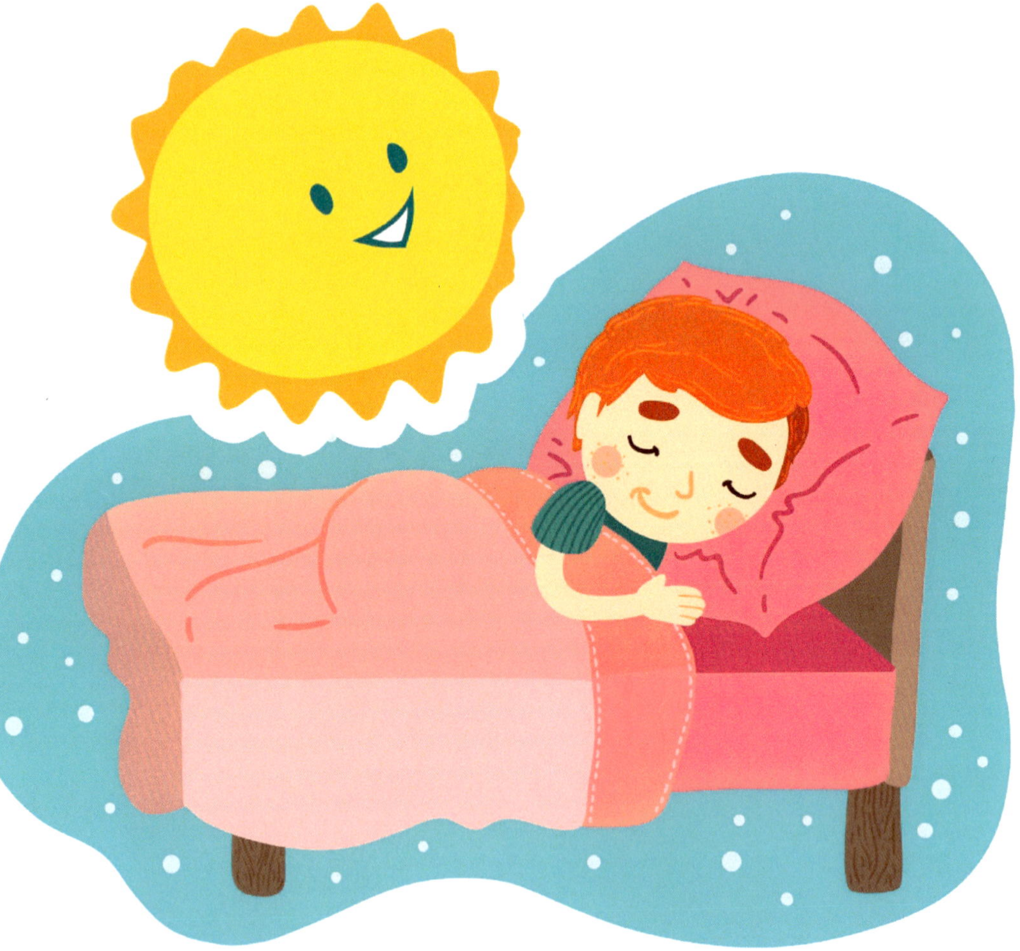

Good morning Sun

Our Day has just Begun

We love to see your shining face

Good morning Sun

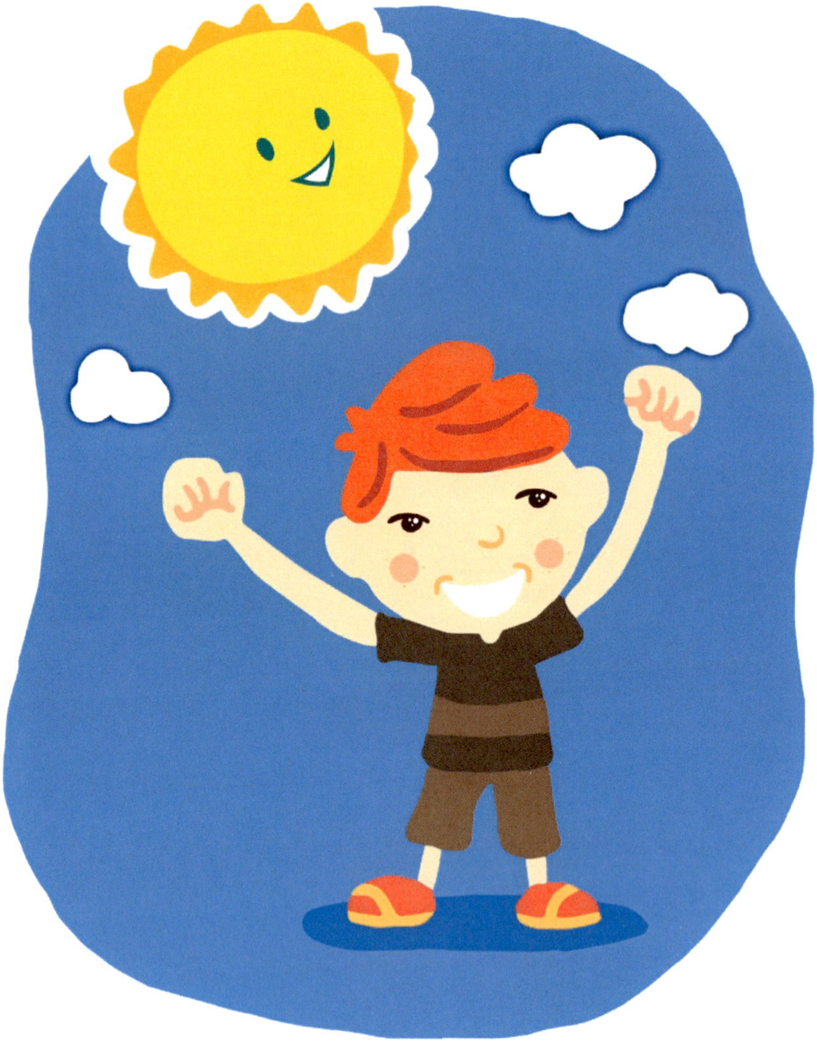

when I get up in the morning
I'll tell you what I Do

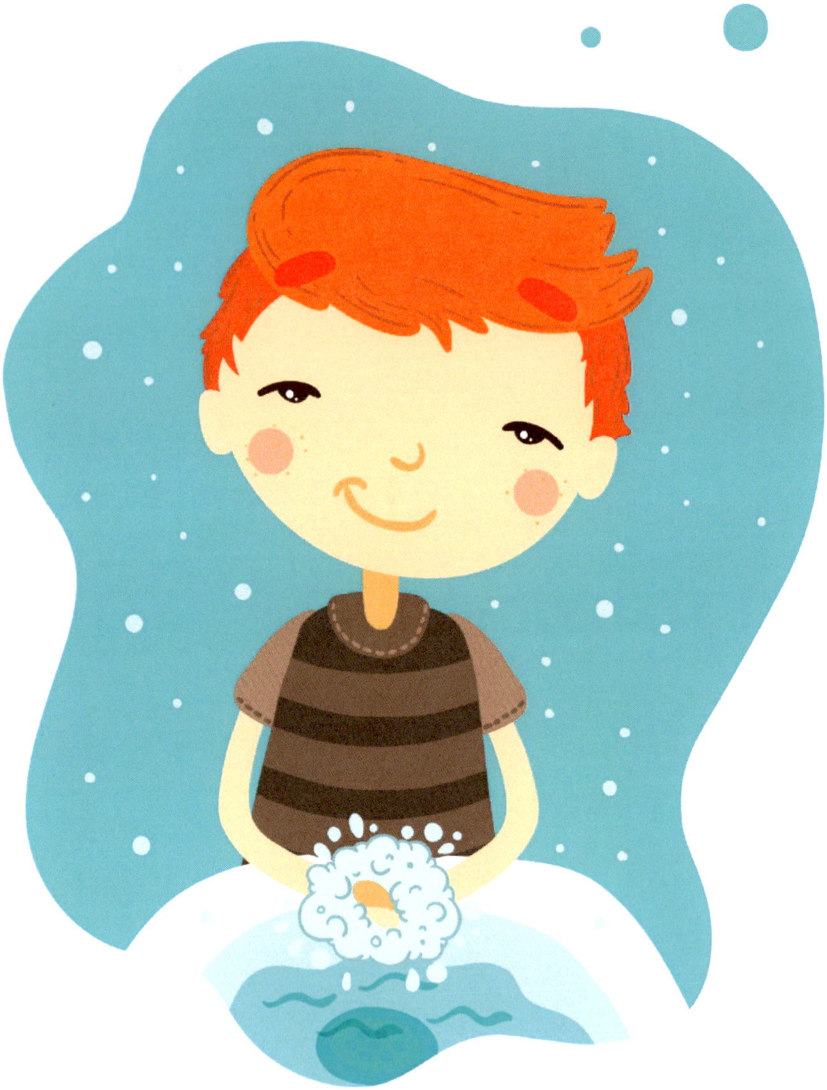

I wash my hands
splishety-splash, splishety-splash

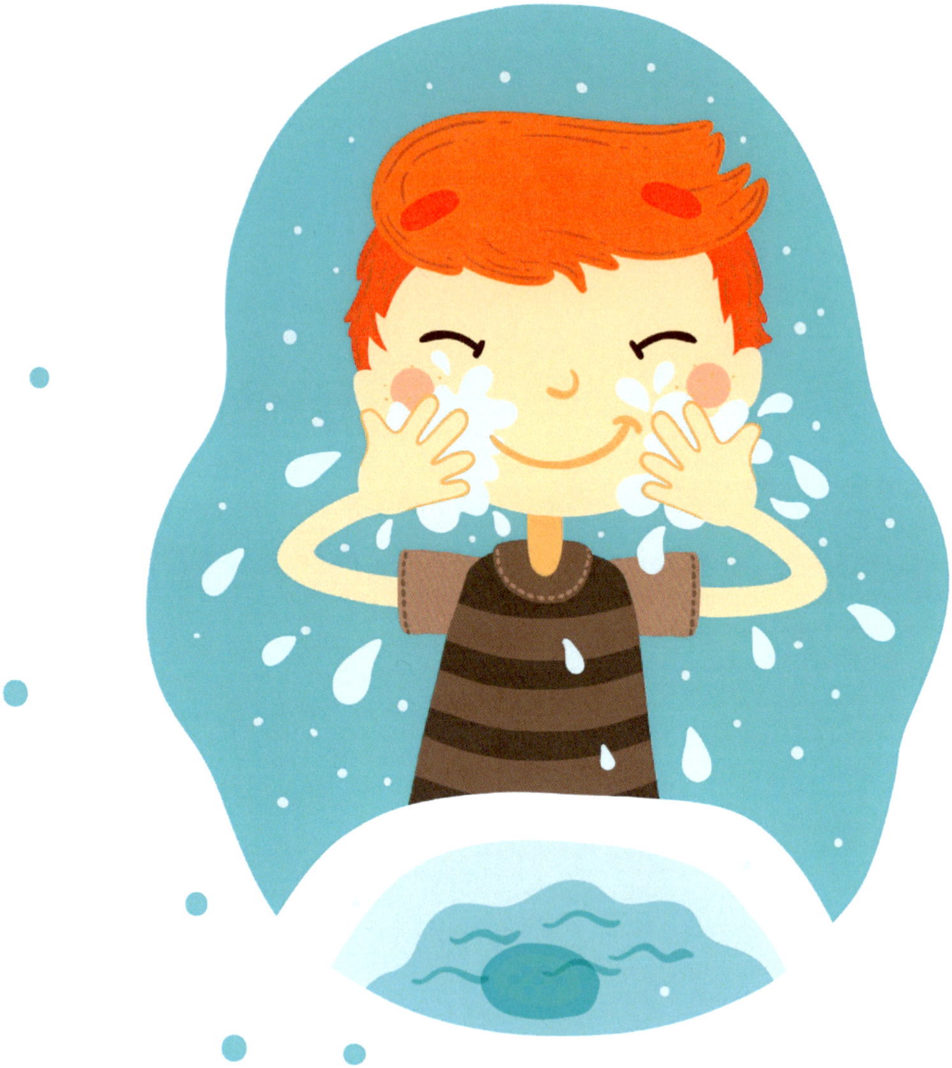

And wash my face
Splishety-splash, splishety-splash

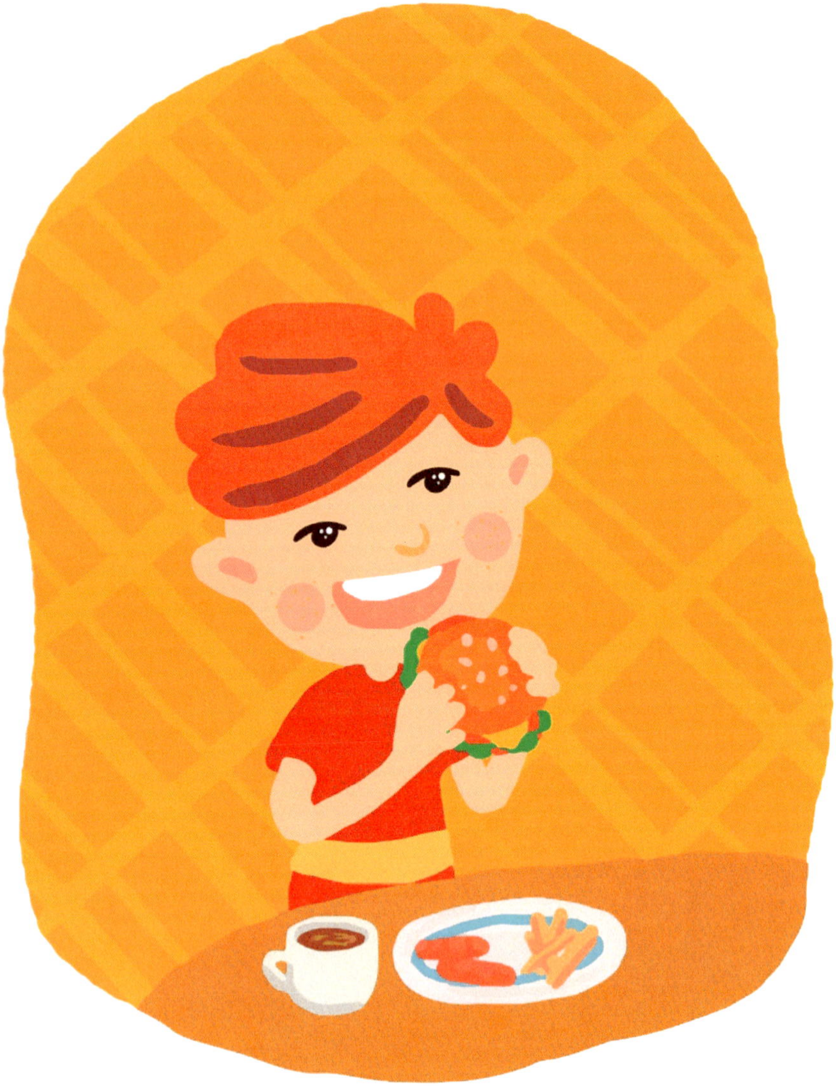

AnD after I go eating my lovely Breakfast

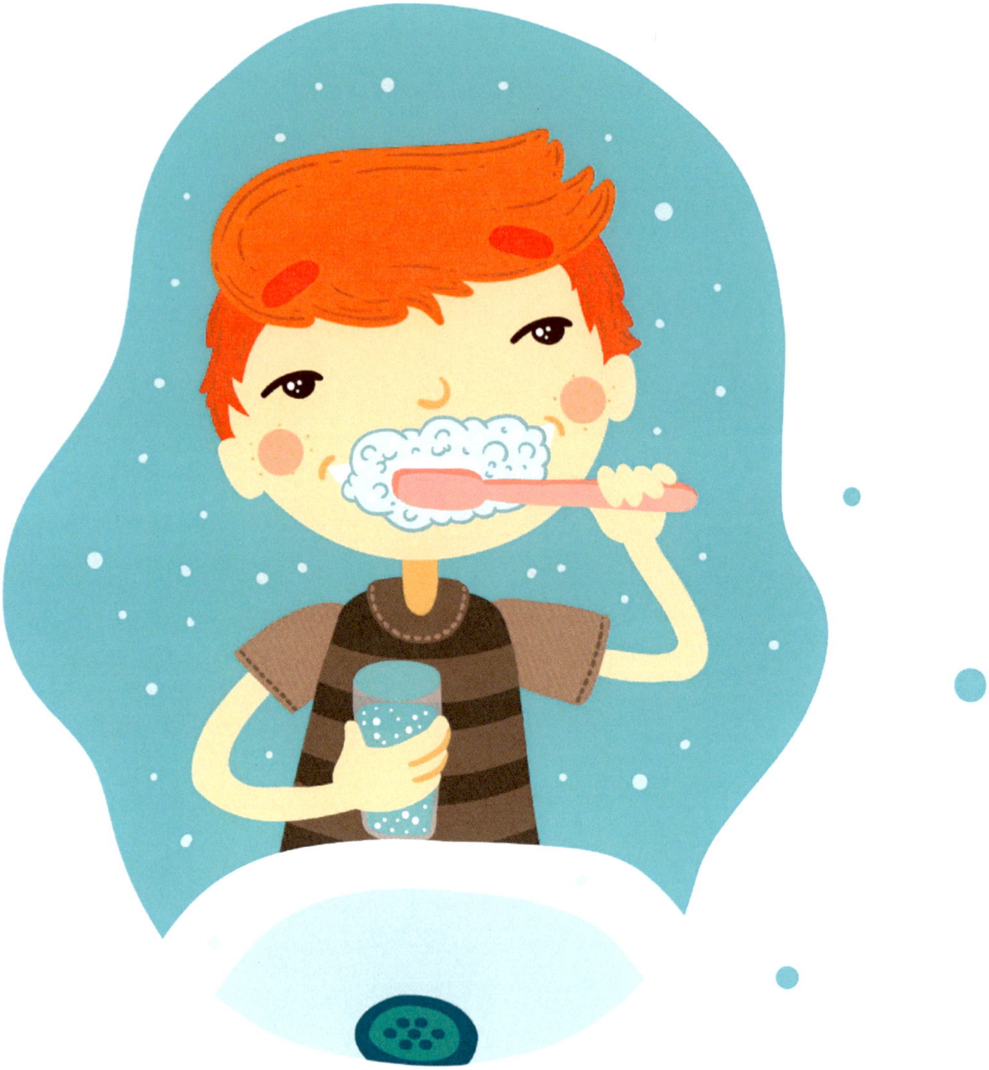

I clean my teeth
till they're shining white
scrubbity-scrub, scrubbity-scrub

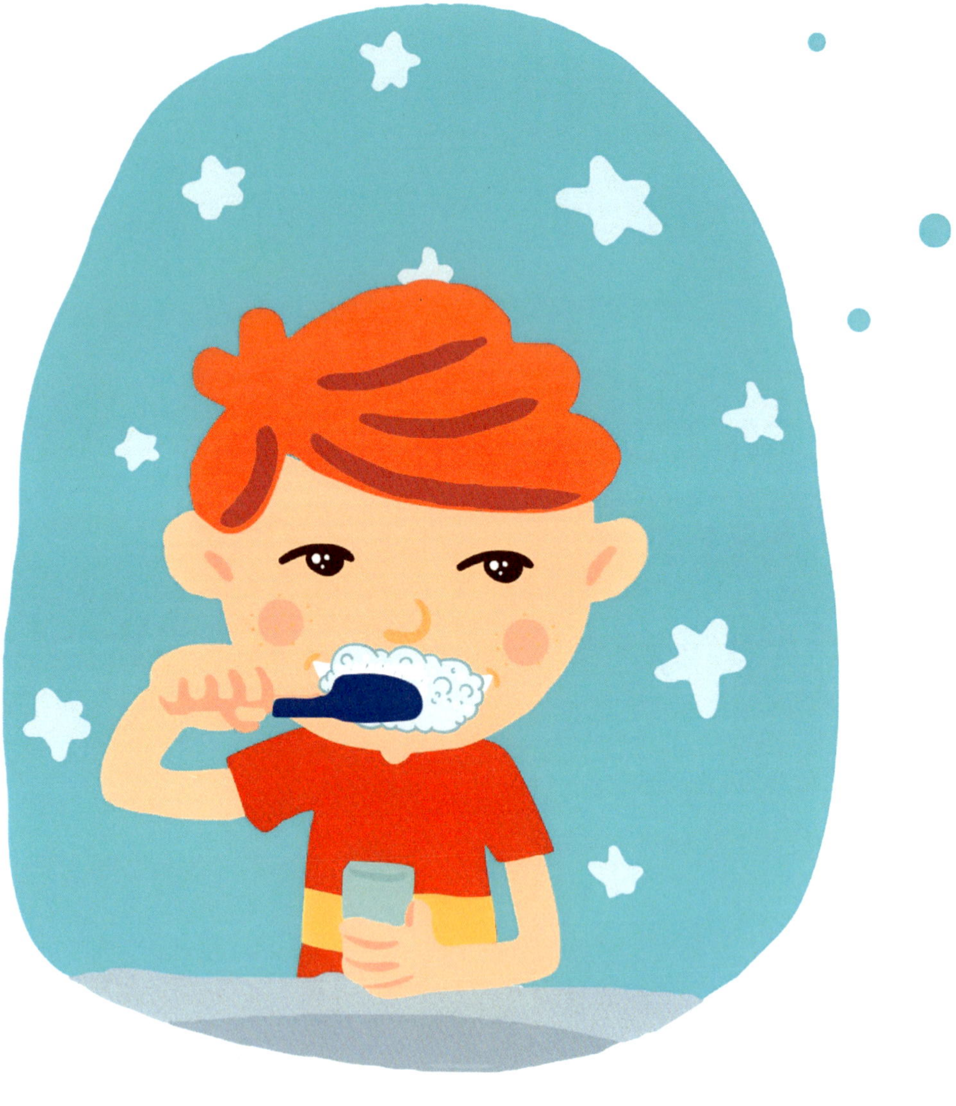

Got my toothpaste, got my brush,
I won't hurry, I won't rush.
Making sure my teeth are clean,
Front and back and in between.

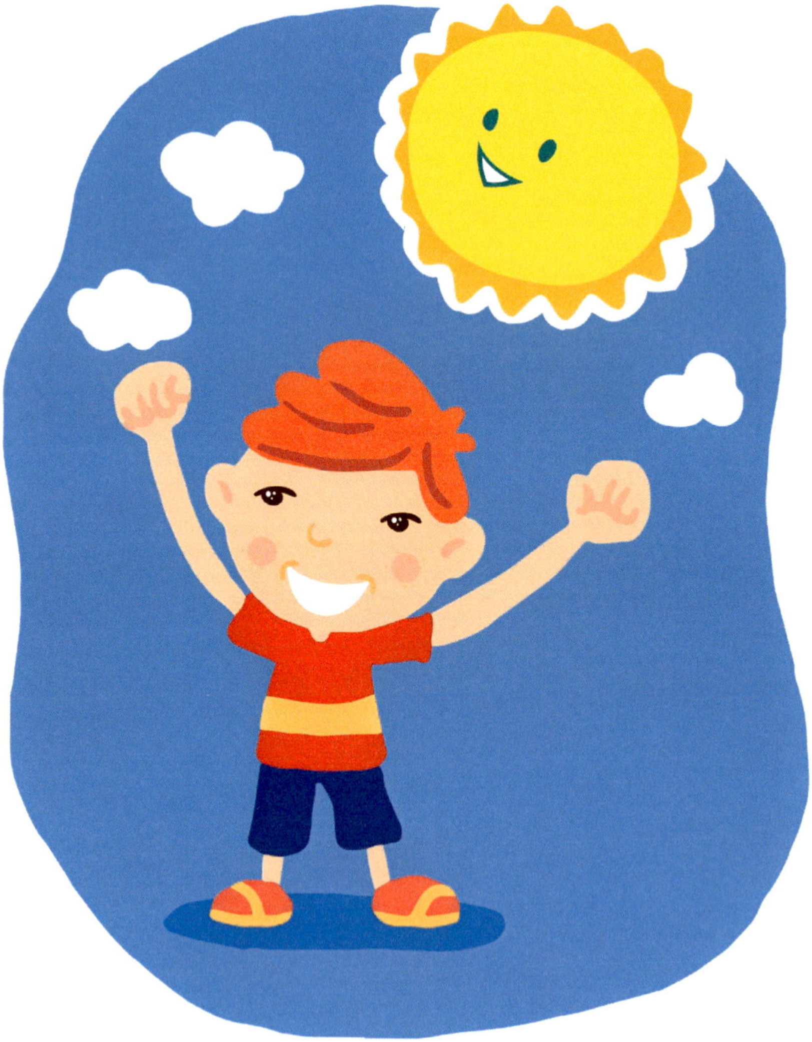

When I brush for quite a while,
I will have a happy smile!

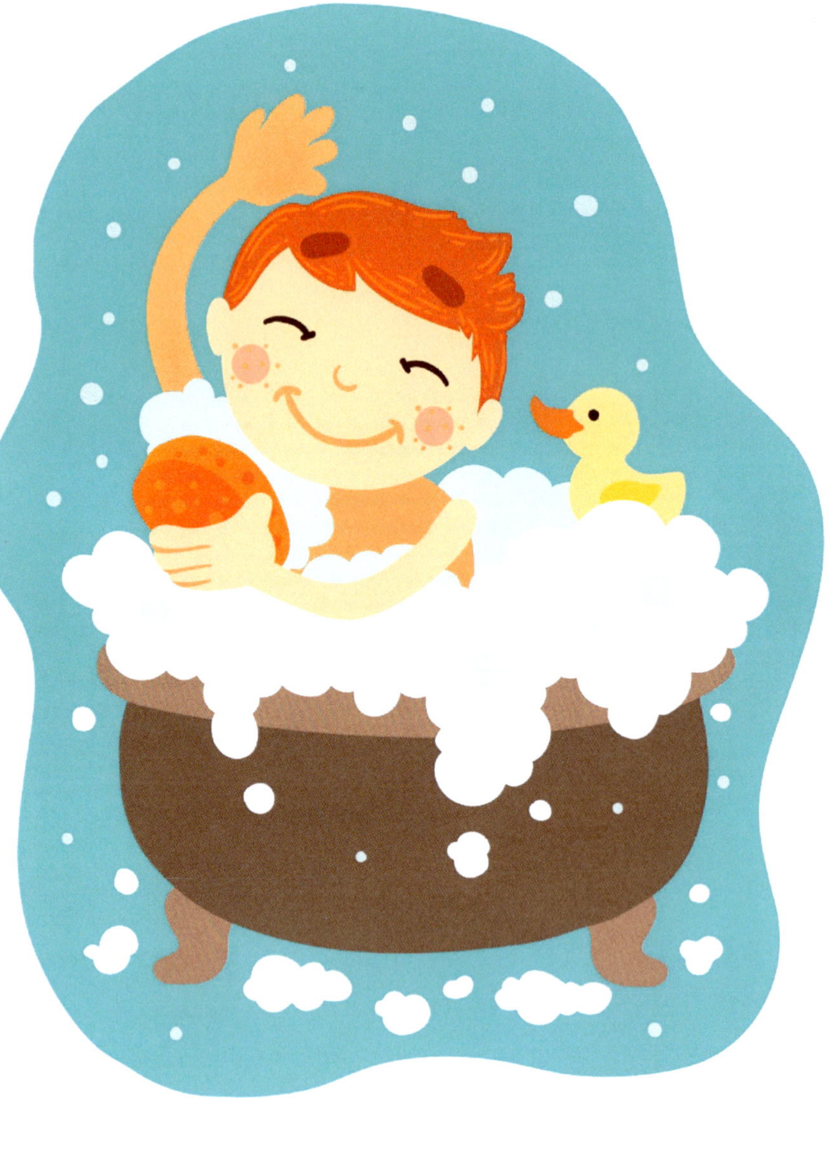

And runnity-run, I run to my bath
I wash my body and my eyes
Splishety-splash, splishety-splash

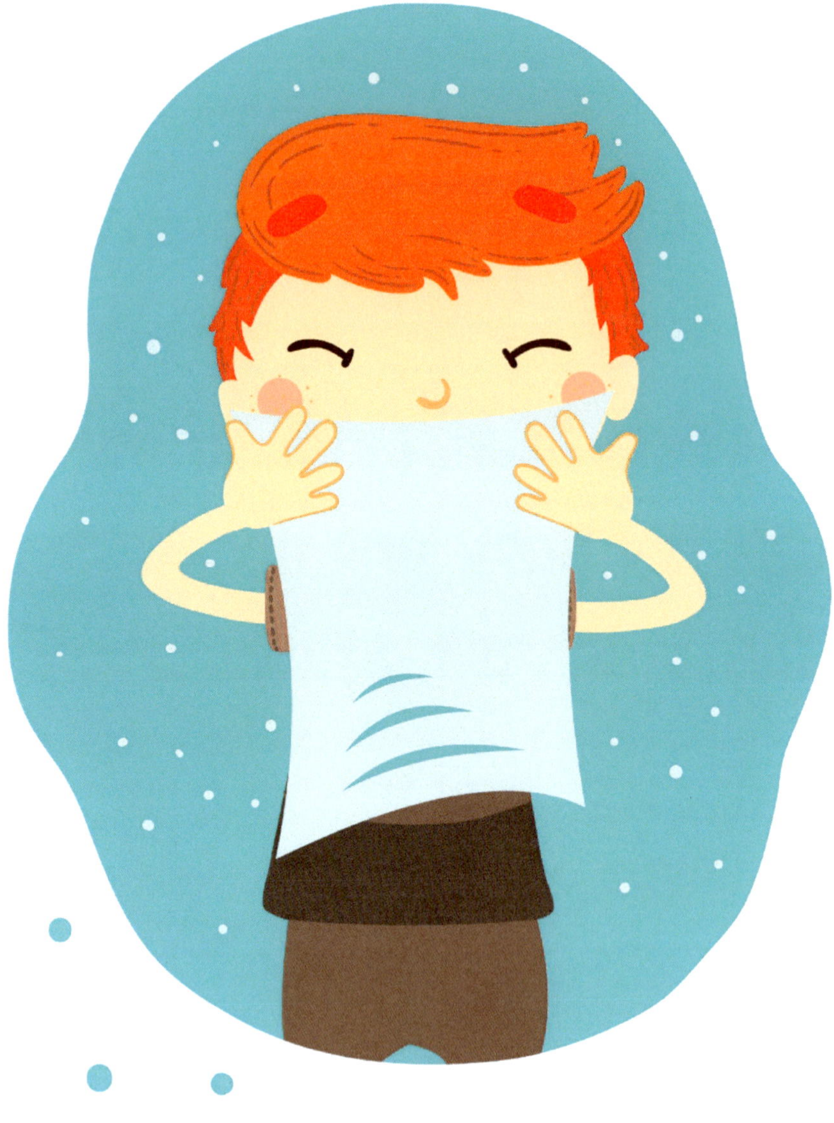

After my Bath, I try, try, try
to wipe myself 'till I'm Dry, Dry, Dry.
Hands to wipe
and fingers and toes
and two wet legs
and a shiny nose.

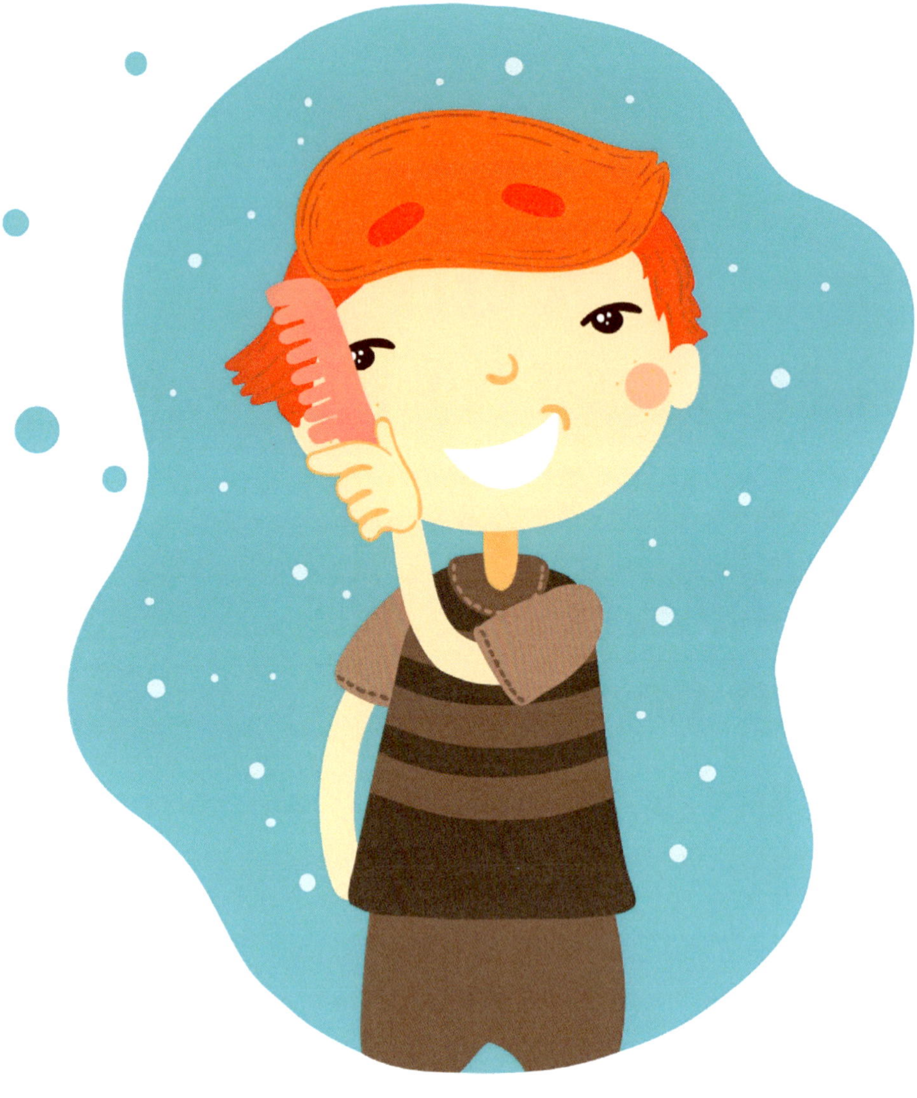

Then I put on my clothes and Brush my hair

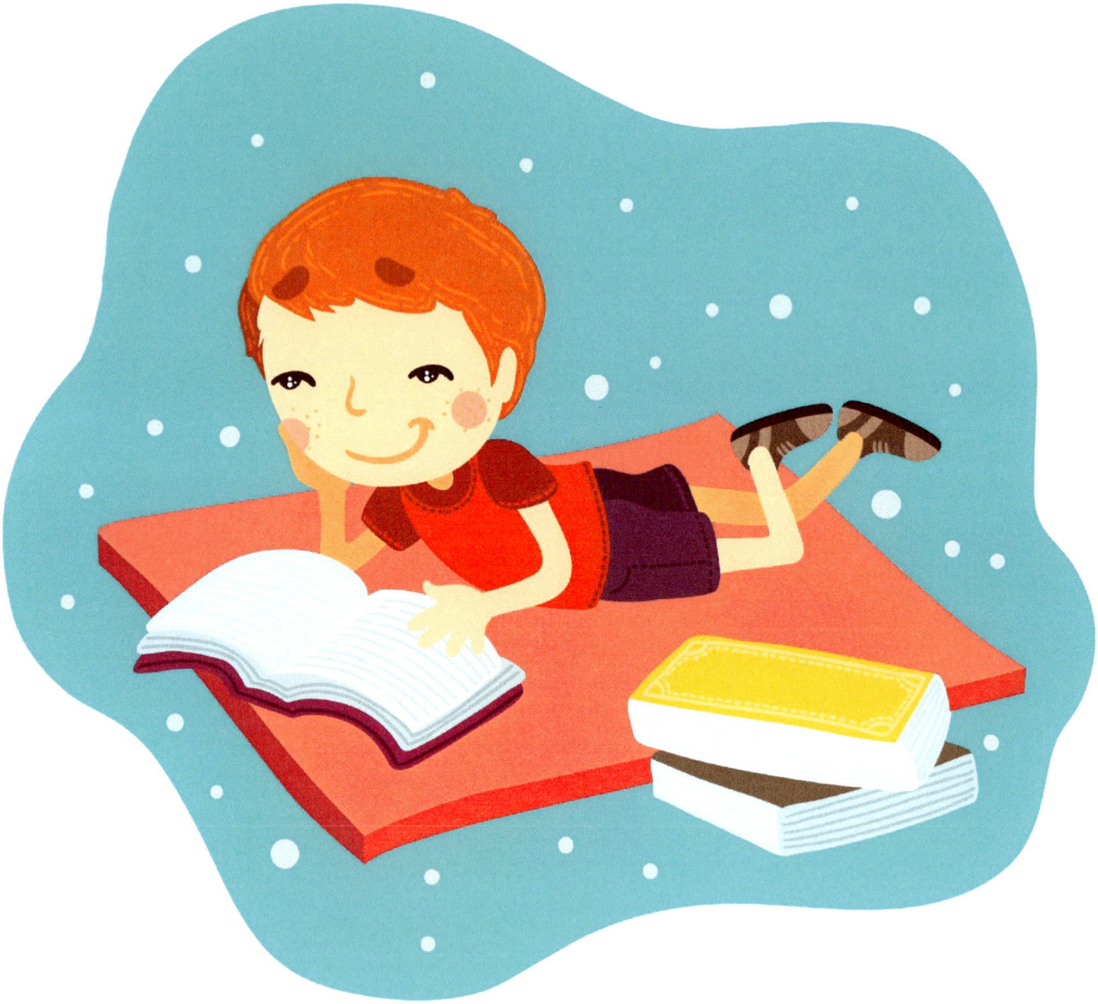

And now I can go to read my adventure story Books

Now available on amazon - save up to 80%
or visit our website: www.provactoshop.com

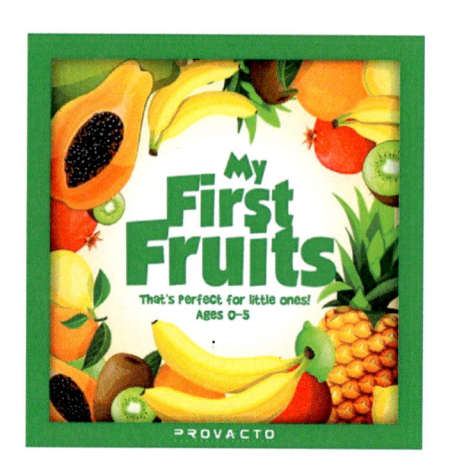

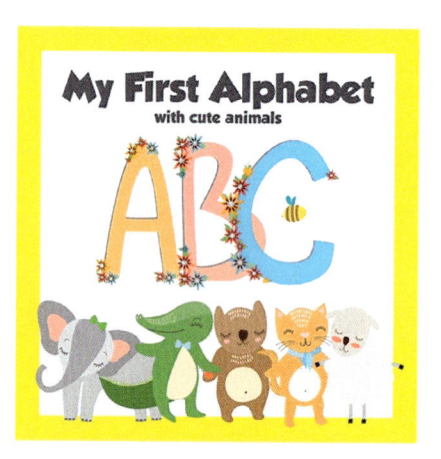

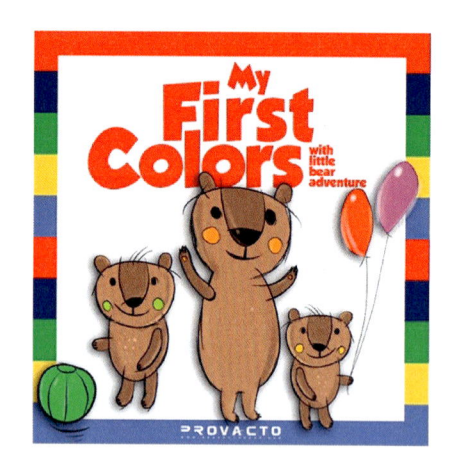

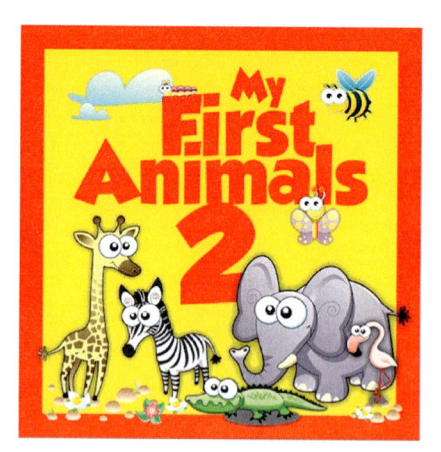

PROVACTO
WWW.PROVACTOSHOP.COM

Now available on amazon - save up to 80%
or visit our website: www.provactoshop.com

PROVACTO
WWW.PROVACTOSHOP.COM

Made in the USA
Lexington, KY
26 January 2018